The Prophecy

V Ö L U S P Á

# *The*
# PROPHECY

The Prophecy of the Vikings –
The Creation of the World

GUDRUN
2001

The Prophecy © GUDRUN 2001

www.gudrunpublishing.com

English translation © Bernard Scudder

Illustrations by Dagfinn Werenskiold © Dagfinn Werenskiold/Bono

Preface, synopsis, characters © Björn Jónasson

Design: Björn Jónasson & Helgi Hilmarsson

ISBN 9979-856-26-2 (Hard cover)
ISBN 9979-856-27-0 (Paperback)

Printed in Iceland
by Oddi Ltd. Printing Press
www.oddi.is

# Contents

# Preface

**The poem**

The Prophecy (*Völuspá*) is the most homogeneous account of the creation of the world according to the ancient faith of the North. It is also one of the most beautiful poems preserved from the Viking Age. Where and when the poem was composed is not known for certain, but there is general agreement among those who have studied The Prophecy that it is completely Scandinavian in character and composed somewhere in Scandinavia, hardly before the year 700 and hardly later than 1000.

Delivered by a prophetess, the poem describes her vision of both past and future. When the poem opens she is sitting at the feet of the Great Father (Odin) and sees the time when nothing existed. Then she recounts how the gods and men came into being, their initially innocent and joyful life, conflicts between different deities, the destruction of the world and, finally, the rebirth of the world.

The poem is preserved complete in two medieval Icelandic manuscripts. The version in the manuscript known as the Codex Regius, thought to have been written down in the thirteenth century, is generally preferred as the better of the two, and is followed here for the main part.

The publisher would like to thank Dr. Terry Gunnell of the University of Iceland for his suggestions and advice.

# Synopsis

### Creation

In the first verse (*A hearing*) the Prophetess asks for silence so that she can tell her vision, and the story of how the world began, to Odin – or the Father of the Fallen as he is referred to here, one of the many names he assumes throughout the poem. Perhaps repeating lore learnt from the giants and ogresses who raised her (*I remember giants*), she relates the origin of the world when nothing had been created and everything was a vast void (*At the dawn of ages*). Then Odin and his brothers (*The First-Born's sons*) arrived to make the Earth, and the sun shone from the south. The sun, moon and stars were still uncertain of their places and functions (*The sun did not know*). The gods convened to allocate tasks to the heavenly bodies and arranged the hours of the day and night (*They called them morning and mid-day*). After that, the gods made a dwelling-place for themselves and made tools for themselves to work with (*On Ever-Green Plain*). Happiness and well-being reigned (*Happiness reigned*), and lasted until the three maidens of fate from the land of the giants made their entrance, as described later on. Needing craftsmen, the gods sought to create a dwarf who would spawn a lineage of toolmakers (*Holy gods in consultation*). The gods then made numerous dwarfs from earth (*The dwarfs*). The earliest manuscript inserts a tally of dwarfs at this point, but there has been some question about whether it was part of the original poem. This interpolation is therefore omitted from the main body of the text in this version, but is printed separately in Appendix II.

Three gods – Odin, Haenir and Lod – find the lifeless forms of Ash and Elm, the first man and first woman, on the shore and breathe life into them (*Ash and Elm* and *Breath and spirit*).


## The world
The Prophetess describes the tree Yggdrasill standing ever-green in the centre of the world. Dew from it drips into the valleys of the Earth, and maidens daub it with white clay (*An ash named Yggdrasill*). From the spring at the tree's roots come the three Fates: Past, Present and Future. They determine the course of people's lives and ordain their fates (*The maidens of fate*).


## Primal conflict
Next, the Prophetess remembers when Gold-Potion, perhaps symbolizing the temptations of gold, visited the gods. Although the gods try to vanquish this corrupting force by stabbing her with spears and burning her, evil is resilient and she rises from the dead at once (*Three times burnt, three times born*). In the next verse (*Cherished by evil women*), reborn as Bright-as-Gold, she is versed in magic and a dangerous adversary. Perhaps it is greed that brings about the downfall of the gods; they convene to decide

whether to make war on the forces that oppose them (*Retribution*). The primal battle is witnessed when the gods and the Vanir clash (*The first battle*), prompted by trickery and slander. An allusion is made to the abduction of the goddess Freyja by the giants (*Deceit*).

Thor resolutely urges the gods to do battle. Oaths and pledges are made (*Thor, the fighter*). The omniscient prophetess knows what Heimdall can hear and what Odin can see. In the Prose Edda (another viking age account of the creation of the world), Heimdall is said to have had such acute hearing that he was posted to guard the bridge to Asgard, the fortress of the gods. This bridge, Bifrost, can sometimes be seen from the world of men, in the form of a rainbow (*What Heimdall hears*). Odin gave one of his eyes as a pledge in return for a drink from Mimir's well, the well of wisdom (*Mimir's well*). The prophetess could tell Odin of things which had not yet come to pass and tidings from other worlds (*She saw far and wide*). In the distance she saw valkyries, an unfailing sign that battle was looming. Valkyries would ride across battlefields, choosing slain heroes to sit with the gods in Valhalla where they would fight all day but rise anew every night to feast and make merry (*The valkyries*).


## The death of Balder

All the gods loved Balder, who symbolized all things good. Disturbed by an intuition about Balder's death, his father Odin made a pact with all things in nature not to cause him harm. But

Odin overlooked a single plant: the seemingly harmless mistletoe, which he could not imagine being used to make a weapon. Hod was the god who symbolizes strength and vigour, and was blind as well. The gods amused themselves by having Hod shoot his bow at Balder, knowing that all the missiles would deflect from him. Loki, the evil god, slipped an arrow made of mistletoe into Hod's bow, and Balder was killed by it. Odin was consumed by the urge to take revenge, and he begat another son to avenge Balder's death and ease the sorrow that he and his wife Frigg felt at their loss (*The fate of Balder, A fatal arrow* and *Frigg's lamentation*). Loki was captured, fettered and left lying where poison dripped from a spring onto his body as a perpetual torture. Sigyn, Loki's wife, came to his aid by catching the drops of poison in a bowl as they fell. When the bowl fills up and she needs to empty it, the poison drips onto Loki's body, and his spasms are felt as earthquakes (*The wily Loki*).

**Destruction unleashed**
The Prophetess looks all about and can see into dark worlds: A river falls from the east through poisonous valleys, full of swords and daggers; she sees halls on the Plains of Darkness and the Shore of the Dead, she sees serpents spewing poison (*The poisoned valleys, The giant's beer-hall, On the Shore of the Dead*). Oath-breakers, pledge-breakers, seducers, murderers and robbers wade through the waters; a dragon sucks the blood of the dead and a wolf gorges on the

11

bodies of men (*Dark-Striker*). She sees an ogress in a forest of iron give birth to a wolf-child which will later swallow the sun itself (*Iron-Wood*). The forces of death magnify, everything is stained with blood and the sunshine turns black (*Black sunshine*).

Now three roosters howl – one in the world of men, another in the world of the gods, and the third in the underworld (*Fjalar, Golden-Comb* and the crimson rooster). A dog barks at the mouth of a cave, and the wolf Fenrir breaks free. Fenrir was so dangerous that the only fetter the gods could make strong enough to tie it down was from the sinews of a bear, the beard of a woman, the roots of a mountain, the breath of a fish, the spirit of a bird and the footsteps of a cat. But amidst all these upheavals, the wolf breaks loose (*Garm barks loud*).


### The doom of the gods

Brothers will fight, the age of swords and storms will dawn and no one will spare the lives of others (*A storm-age, a wolf-age*), the Prophetess foretells. Heimdall sounds his horn, the Gjallar-horn, which can be heard throughout the world calling the gods to battle (*Fate is kindled*). Beneath the plodding footsteps of the giant, the tree of life, Yggdrasill, trembles. (*The giant breaks loose*). And the dog Garm barks again (*Garm barks by Gaping-Cave*).

Hrym the giant approaches from the east and the Midgard Serpent thrashes around in a frenzy. The pale-beaked eagle feeds on corpses and Nail-Ship, made from the fingernails and toenails of the dead, breaks free from its moorings. A band of giants led by Muspell and the evil Loki steer the ship, and the chaos builds up to a climax. Surt (fire) enters, burning everything in his path, men plunge to hell and the heavens are split apart (*The serpent writhes in fury, The kin of folly, What's with the gods* and *Surt comes with fire*).

### The ultimate battle

Odin, husband of Hlin (also named Frigg), does battle with the wolf and dies. Frey, the slayer of Beli, tackles Surt (*Odin fights the wolf*). And the dog barks yet again (*Garm barks....*). Odin's son Vidar comes forth and kills the wolf Fenrir (*Vidar avenges Odin*). Thor engages in a mighty battle with the Midgard Serpent, ending with the deaths of both (*Thor and the serpent*). The sun turns black, the land sinks into the sea and the stars are extinguished in the sky. Tongues of flame lick the heavens and the dog barks yet again (*The sun turns black* and *The mighty doom*).

### Resurrection

When the catastrophe is over at last, the Prophetess sees the Earth rise from the sea anew. Waterfalls cascade and eagles swoop down to hunt from the mountainsides (*The Earth arises a second time*). And the gods meet again to recall the awesome serpent and the mighty deeds of old (*The gods meet again*). The Prophetess foretells that the gods' golden chessmen will be retrieved (*Golden chessmen*). She sees unsown fields grow and prophesies the lifting of all sorrow, and she sees Balder return, reconciled now with the blind god Hod in Valhalla. The offspring of the gods will dwell in comfort in the heavens (*The return of Balder* and *The winds' domain*). She also sees a hall more beautiful than the sun where the worthiest of men will stay for ever after (*Fairer than the sun*). But, ominously, the terrible black dragon still lurks in the background (*Again Dark-Striker*).

# The Prophecy

## *A  hearing*

A hearing I ask
of all humankind,
the higher and lower
kin of Heimdall;
They, Father of the Fallen,
wanted me to recount
the ancient deeds of heroes
I recall from time's dawn.

## *I remember giants*

I remember giants
born of yore
who long ago
reared and raised me;
nine worlds I recall,
nine ogresses,
the famed tree of fate
beneath the earth.

## *At the dawn of ages*

At the dawn of ages
there was nothing,
neither sand nor sea
nor cool waves:
earth was found nowhere
nor the heavens above,
only the great void
and nowhere grass.

## *The First-Born's sons*

Until the First-Born's sons
arched up the lands,
makers of Midgard,
famed Middle Earth.
Sun shone from the south
on the rock-built earth,
then the ground was grown
with green plants.

## *The sun did not know*

The sun shed from the south,
the moon's companion,
with its right hand over
the rim of the sky.
The sun did not know
where to seek repose,
the stars did not know
where they could rest,
the moon did not know
what might it had.

## They called them morning and mid-day

Then all the powers met
who mete out fate,
mighty, holy gods
in consultation:
to night and its offspring
they gave names,
called them morning
and mid-day,
afternoon and evening,
to be counted in years.

## On Ever-Green Plain

The High Ones met
on Ever-Green Plain,
they who raised timbered
shrines and temples,
built furnaces,
wrought precious things,
made tongs
and forged tools.

### *Happiness reigned*

Happily they played
chess in the meadow,
they lacked for nothing
made of gold;
until three maidens
of the giants came,
full of force
from the World of Giants.

*Holy gods in consultation*

Then all the powers met
who mete out fate,
mighty, holy gods
in consultation:
on which one should make
the master of the dwarfs
from Sea-Swell's blood
and blue legs.

## *The dwarfs*

Thus Sea-Mind
most renowned became
of all the dwarfs,
Dwarfish was second;
they made many
human forms,
the dwarfs from earth,
as Dwarfish told them...

### Ash and Elm

... until three mighty
and impassioned gods
from that band
approached the dwelling.
On the shore they found
Ash and Elm,
capable of little,
their fate unformed.

### Breath and spirit

They had no breath,
they had no spirit,
neither warmth nor voice
nor fine complexion.
Odin gave them breath,
Haenir gave them spirit,
Lod gave them warm life
and fine complexion.

## *An ash named Yggdrasill*

I know an ash stands,
named Yggdrasill,
a high tree, washed
with white clay;
from it come the dews
that fall in the valleys,
it stands ever-green
over Spring of the Past.

## The maidens of fate

From there come
the much-knowing maidens,
three from the sea
that lies under the tree:
one was named Past,
another Present
– they carved in wood –
and Future the third;
they laid down the law,
they chose lives
for the children of men,
people's fates.

## *Three times burnt,*
## *three times born*

She remembers the onslaught
of the world's first battle,
when Gold-Potion
was pierced with spears
and in High One's hall
she was burnt.
Three times burnt,
three times born,
often, unseldom,
yet still she lives.

*Cherished by evil women*

Bright-as-Gold they called her
wherever she visited,
a seeress far-sighted,
she conjured with wands,
in magic she was versed,
in magic she was deft,
always she was cherished
by the evil women.

## Retribution

Then all the powers met
who mete out fate,
mighty, holy gods
in consultation:
as to whether the high ones
should suffer that scourge
or the gods should all
seek retribution.

*The first battle*

Odin hurled down
and shot over the warriors,
that was yet the onslaught
of the world's first battle,
the stockades were broken
of the High Ones' fortress,
the Vanir stamped the ground
with their chants of battle.

## Deceit

Then all the powers met
who mete out fate,
mighty, holy gods
in consultation:
as to who had poisoned
the air with deceit,
or given Od's bride
to the race of giants.

## Thor, the fighter

Thor alone there
was stirred to fight
– he seldom lingers
when he hears such things –
oaths were breached,
words and pledges,
weighty were the statements
that passed among them.

## What Heimdall hears

She knows that what Heimdall
hears is hidden
under the sacred tree
that spreads to the heavens.
She sees a river pouring
in a muddy fall from the eye
pledged by the Father of the Fallen.
Would you know more – or not?

## Mimir's well

Alone she sat outside
when the Old One came,
forebear of the gods
and looked her in the eye.
What do you ask me to tell?
Why do you tempt me?
– I know it all, Odin,
where you hid your eye,
within Mimir's
much-famed well.
Mimir drinks the mead
every morning from the eye
pledged by the Father of the Fallen.
Would you know more – or not?

*She saw far and wide*

The War-Father chose for her
brooches and necklaces,
wealth, words of wisdom
and divinations,
she saw far and wide
into every world.

## The valkyries

She saw valkyries
arrive from afar,
ordained to ride
to the race of the gods:
Future held a shield,
Prodder was another,
War, Battle, Weaver
and Spear-Prodder.
Now they are counted,
the Warmaker's handmaids,
valkyries ordained
to ride the ground.

## *The fate of Balder*

I saw fate
allotted to Balder,
the blood-stained deity,
child of Odin;
there it stood, grown
higher than the plains,
slender and beautiful
the mistletoe.

## *A fatal arrow*

From that tree was made
a fatal arrow of sorrow
though slight it seemed:
Hod shot it.
A brother was born
early to Balder,
Odin's son avenged
when one night old.

## Frigg's lamentation

He never washed his hands
nor combed his hair
before Balder's adversary
was borne to his pyre;
in the Fen-Hall
Frigg lamented the doom
done in Valhalla.
Would you know more – or not?

### *The wily Loki*

She saw a bound form lying
under the grove of springs
resembling the body
of wily Loki;
Sigyn sat there
not full of glee
about her husband.
Would you know more – or not?

## The poisoned valleys

A river falls from the east
through poisoned valleys
full of daggers and swords,
Scabbard is its name.

## *The giant's beer-hall*

To the north stood
on the Plains of Darkness
a hall of gold,
the legacy of dwarfs;
another stood
on Ever-Warm,
the giant's beer-hall,
his name is Sea-Swell.

## On the Shore of the Dead

She saw a hall standing
far from the sun
on the Shore of the Dead,
its door facing north.
Drops of poison
drip in through the hatch,
that hall is entwined
with the ridged backs of serpents.

## *Dark-Striker*

There she saw wading
mighty currents
men of ill oath
and murderous scavengers
and the beguiler of another's
whisperer of secrets;
Dark-Striker sucked there
on corpses of the departed,
a wolf tore up men.
Would you know more – or not?

## *Iron-Wood*

In the east the old ogress
sat in Iron-Wood
and there gave birth
to the wolf's offspring.
Of them, a certain
one will be made
to devour the sun
in a trollish guise.

## Black sunshine

The wolf fills with the force
of men fated to die,
smears with red blood
the gods' heavenly site,
the sunshine was black
for summers after,
the weather treacherous.
Would you know more – or not?

## *Eggther and Fjalar*

He sat on a mound there
and smote his harp,
the ogress's herder,
gleeful Eggther.
Howling to him
in the nesting reeds
a bright red rooster,
its name Fjalar.

## *Golden-Comb*

To the gods it howled,
Golden-Comb,
who rouses the heroes
of the Warring Father.
But another howls
beneath the earth,
a crimson rooster,
in the halls of Hell.

## *Garm barks loud*

Garm barks loud
by Gaping-Cave,
the fetter will break
and the wolf run free;
lore she knows in plenty,
I see beyond the future,
the mighty doom
of the triumphant gods.

# *A storm-age, a wolf-age*

Brothers will do battle
unto the death,
sons of sisters
fight their own kin,
the world has turned harsh,
great fornication,
an axe-age, a sword-age,
shields are cleft,
a storm-age, a wolf-age,
before the world tumbles
no man will ever
spare another.

## *Fate is kindled*

Mimir's sons play,
while fate is kindled
by the blaring
Gjallarhorn;
Heimdall blows loud,
his horn aloft,
Odin speaks
to Mimir's head.

*The giant breaks loose*

The ancient tree groans
and the giant breaks loose;
still standing, the ash
Yggdrasill trembles.

## *Garm barks by Gaping-Cave*

Garm barks loud now
by Gaping-Cave,
the fetter will break
and the wolf run free;
lore she knows in plenty,
I see beyond the future,
the mighty doom
of the triumphant gods.

## The serpent writhes in fury

Hrym drives from the east,
his shield before him,
the mighty serpent writhes
in gigantic fury.
The snake thrashes the waves
and the eagle grows joyful,
pale-beak plucks corpses,
Nail-Ship breaks its moorings.

## The kin of folly

The ship comes from the east,
Muspell's band of giants
will cross the seas
with Loki steering,
all the kin of folly
will go with the wolf,
Byleip's brother
faring with them.

## *What's with the gods?*

What's with the gods?
What's with the elves?
All the World of Giants rumbles,
the High Ones convene,
dwarfs groan
by their doors of rock,
the wise cliff-dwellers.
Would you know more – or not?

## Surt comes with fire

Surt comes from the south
with his wood-eating fire,
sun glints on the sword
of the godly warriors.
Boulders slam together,
sending trolls tumbling,
men tread the path to Hell
and the heavens cleave.

## *Odin fights the wolf*

Then comes to pass
Hlin's second woe,
when Odin goes forth
to fight the wolf,
and Beli's bright slayer
to face Surt;
Frigg's beloved god
will fall dead then.

## *Garm barks by Gaping-Cave*

Garm barks loud now
by Gaping-Cave,
the fetter will break
and the wolf run free;
lore she knows in plenty,
I see beyond the future,
the mighty doom
of the triumphant gods.

## *Vidar avenges Odin*

Then comes the great son
of Victory-Father,
Vidar, to smite
the carrion beast.
With his hand he thrusts
his spear through the heart
of Rager's son,
avenging a father.

## Thor and the serpent

Then comes the famed
son of mother Earth,
Odin's son goes forth
to fight the beast,
Midgard's keeper
hammers the serpent.
All men strip clear
their homes in the world,
Earth's progeny moves
nine steps back
and perishes by the serpent
unfearful of reproach.

### The sun turns black

The sun turns black,
land sinks into sea,
the bright stars
vanish from the sky.
Fire rages forth
at the life-giving tree,
high flame will lick
at heaven itself.

## *The mighty doom*

Garm barks loud now
by Gaping-Cave,
the fetter will break
and the wolf run free;
lore she knows in plenty,
I see beyond the future,
the mighty doom
of the triumphant gods.

## *The Earth arises a second time*

She sees arise
a second time
Earth from the sea,
ever-green.
Water cascades,
the eagle soars above,
catcher of fish
on the mountains' sides.

## *The gods meet again*

The gods meet again
on Ever-Green Plain,
reflect on the mighty
earth-curling serpent
and recall there
those ultimate deeds
and the ancient secrets
of the Greatest God's runes.

## *Golden chessmen*

Later will be found
wondrously wrought
golden chessmen
in the grass there,
which in days of yore
they had owned.

## The return of Balder

Unsown fields
will grow up then,
all sorrow will be lifted,
Balder will return.
Hod and Balder will thrive,
gods in the ruins
of the Hailer's hall.
Would you know more – or not?

## The winds' domain

Then Haenir will choose
the soothsaying wood
and the sons of the two
brothers will dwell
in the wide winds' domain:
Would you know more – or not?

## *Fairer than the sun*

She sees a hall standing
fairer than the sun
bedecked with gold
leeward of the fire.
Men of worth
will dwell there,
delighting in it
for ever after.

## Ruler of all things

*Then the wielder*
*of godly power*
*descends in might,*
*ruler of all things.*

## Again Dark-Striker

There the dim dragon
will come in flight,
the glittering serpent,
from Dark Mountains below.
Bearing corpses in its feathers,
as it soars over the plain,
the Dark-Striker.
Now she will sink down.

# Appendix I

## Characters

A brief introduction to the heroes and antiheroes of The Prophecy is necessary in order to appreciate the poem in full. Many of the characters are called by more than one name, which in the present translation is often translated literally, to convey some of the mythological force of the original. The characters are:

## The forces of good:

*Aesir (the Gods):*

*Odin*, also named Father of the Fallen, High One, War-Father, War-Maker, the Greatest God, Frigg's beloved god, Victory-Father, forebear of the gods, Hailer

*Thor*, also named son of mother Earth, Odin's son, Midgard's keeper, Earth's progeny

*Heimdall*, the watchguard god, who could hear all things

*Balder*, the good god

*Hod*, the blind god

*Vidar*, also named the son of Victory-Father (son of Odin). Vidar killed the wolf Fenrir

*Haenir*, god of the winds

*Vali*, a god begotten by Odin specifically to avenge Balder

*Lod* (only known from The Prophecy)

*Frigg*, also named Hlin (wife of Odin)

*Sigyn*, wife of Loki

*Sif*, wife of Thor

*Hlodyn*, also named mother Earth (mother of Thor by Odin)

*Vanir (another tribe of gods):*

*Njord*, father of Frey and Freyja,

*Od*, an obscure minor deity

*Frey*

*Freyja*, also named Od's bride

## The forces of evil:
*Giants (also named the kin of folly) and monsters*
    *Ymir*, forefather of the giants
    *Hrym*
    *Sea-Swell* (Brimir)
    *Surt*
    *The giants*
    *Byleip* (Whirlwind?)
    *Beli* (Bully?)
    *Muspell*
    *Three maidens of the giants*
    *Loki*, cunning and evil, who keeps company with
        the gods but is also the cause of their
        downfall; also named Rager (Hvedrung)
    *Fenrir*, a wolf
    *The Midgard Serpent*, also named the mighty
        serpent
    *Dark-Striker* (Nidhogg), a dragon

## Intermediary figures
    *First-Born* (Bur, father of Odin, Vilji and Ve)

*Dwarfs*
    *Sea-Mind* (Motsognir)
    *Dwarfish* (Durinn)
    *Dormant* (Dvalinn)

*Fates*
    *Past* (Urd)
    *Present* (Verdandi)
    *Future* (Skuld)
    *Gold-Potion* (Gullveig, the incarnation of gold).
        Also named *Bright-as-Gold* (Heid)

*Trollwomen*
    *The nine ogresses*

*Valkyries*
    *Prodder* (Skogul)
    *War* (Gunn)
    *Battle* (Hild)
    *Weaver* (Gondul)
    *Spear-Prodder* (Geirskogul)

*Humans*

*Ash* (Ask), the first man

*Elm* (Embla), the first woman

*a man*

*a woman*, mentioned only as "whisperer of secrets"

*Eggther*, a herdsman

## Places and dwellings

*World of Giants (Jotunheimar)*

*Ever-Green Plain (Idavellir)*, meeting-place of the gods

*Fen-Hall*, dwelling of Odin's wife Frigg

*Valhalla (hall of the slain)*, where renowned warriors go after their death, to fight during the day, rise up again and eat and drink at night

*Ever-Warm*, the beer-hall of the giant Sea-Swell

*Plains of Darkness*, place in the world of the dead

*Shore of the Dead*, the coast of Hell

*Iron-Wood*, a forest

*Gaping-Cave*

*Leeward of the Fire* (Gimle), a heavenly place

*Dark Mountains*, home of the giants or a place in the world of the dead

## The world of nature: animals and phenomena

*Spring of the Past*, at the roots of the ash Yggdrasil

*Yggdrasil*, also named the famed tree of fate: the great tree of life which stands in the middle of the Earth

*Mimir's well*, the fountain of wisdom

*Scabbard*, a poisonous river running through the world of the dead

*Fjalar*, a rooster

*Golden-Comb*, a rooster

*Garm*, a dog

*Gjallarhorn*, Heimdall's horn, used to call the gods to battle

*Nail-Ship*, made from the nails of dying men if these are not cut

# Appendix II

The following tally of dwarfs, which various scholars have regarded as a somewhat later addition to the orginal prophecy, occurs in some manuscripts between the verses printed here on pp. 27 and 29. Some of the translations of the names are conjectural. The parallel Icelandic version printed here may be of interest to readers of Tolkein, since he borrowed many of the dwarfs' names for his work.

## Names of Dwarfs

Waxer and Waner,
North and South,
East and West,
All-Thief, Dormant,
Shaker, Shiverer,
Squat, Shorty,
Foreborn, Forebearer,
Forebear, Mead-Wolf.

Nýi og Niði,
Norðri og Suðri,
Austri og Vestri,
Alþjófur, Dvalinn.
Bívör, Bávör,
Bömbur, Nóri,
Án og Ánar,
Ái, Mjöðvitnir.

Force and Wand-Elf,
Wind-Elf, Stubborn,
Darer and Stiff,
Nice, Wise and Coloured,
Corpse and New-Fangled,
Mighty and Wise-Counsel;
Now I have counted
the dwarfs truly.

Veigur og Gandálfur,
Vindálfur, Þráinn,
Þekkur og Þorinn,
Þrór, Vitur og Litur,
Nár og Nýráður,
nú hefi eg dverga,
Reginn og Ráðsviður,
rétt um talda.

Filer, Planer,
Finder, Nailer,
Handle, Toil,
Craftsman, Shrinker,
Swift, Horn-Driller,
Renowned and Drifter,
Swamp, Warrior,
Oaken-Shield.

Fíli, Kíli,
Fundinn, Náli,
Hefti, Víli,
Hanar, Svíur,
Frár, Hornbori,
Frægur og Lóni,
Aurvangur, Jari,
Eikinskjaldi.

page 38
*Vanir*: a rival tribe of gods

page 39
*Od's bride*: Freyja

page 42
*What Heimdall hears*: Heimdall has possibly pledged his hearing here,
    just as Odin pledged one eye to gain wisdom.

page 43
*The Old One*: Odin
*forebear of the gods*: Odin

page 44
*War-Father*: Herfodur = Odin

page 45
*Future*: Skuld
*Prodder*: Skogul
*War*: Gunn
*Battle*: Hild
*Weaver*: Gondul
*Spear-Prodder*: Geirskogul
*Warmaker*: Herjann = Odin

page 48
*A brother to Balder*: Vali, begotten by Odin to avenge Balder

page 49
*Fen-Hall*: home of the goddess Frigg

page 51
*Scabbard*: Slid

page 52
*Plains of Darkness*: Nidavellir
*Ever-Warm*: Okolnir

page 53
*Shore of the Dead*: Nastrond

page 55
*whisperer of secrets*: lover, wife
*Dark-Striker*: Nidhogg (a serpent)

page 56
*Iron-Wood*: Jarnvid
*wolf* = Fenrir

page 59
*Warring Father*: Herjafodur = Odin

page 61
*Garm*: Garm, a dog

*Gaping-Cave*: Gnipahellir

page 63
*Gjallarhorn*: Heimdall's horn

page 66
*mighty serpent*: Midgard Serpent
*snake*: Midgard Serpent
*Nail-Ship*: ship made from the nails of dying men if these are not
    cut
*Hrym*: a giant

page 67
*kin of folly*: giants
*Byleip's brother* (= Whirlwind's brother?): Loki

page 71
*Hlin*: = Frigg, Odin's wife.
*Beli*: (= Bully?), a gaint; his slayer: Frey

page 73
*Victory-Father*: Odin
*carrion beast*: the wolf Fenrir
*Rager*: Hvedrung = Loki, father of the wolf Fenrir

page 75
*mother Earth*: Hlodyn; her and Odin's son: Thor
*Midgard's keeper*: Thor
*Earth's progeny*: Thor

page 76
*life-giving tree*: Yggrasill

page 80
*earth-curling serpent*: Midgard serpent
*greatest god*: Fimbultyr = Odin

page 82
*Hailer*: Odin

page 83
*Haenir*: god of the wind
*sons of the two brothers*: i.e. of Balder and Haenir
*winds' domain*: heavens

page 84
*Leeward of the fire*: Gimle, a name for heaven

page 85
Scholars disagree as to whether or not this verse belongs to the
    original version of the poem.

page 87
*she will sink down*: i.e. the prophetess